THE 10 SECOND KILL ZONE

The Lone Wolf

ISBN: 978-1-4834-5663-8 (sc)
ISBN: 978-1-4834-5664-5 (e)

Because of the dynamic nature of the Internet, any web addresses or
links contained in this book may have changed since publication and
may no longer be valid. The views expressed in this work are solely those
of the author and do not necessarily reflect the views of the publisher,
and the publisher hereby disclaims any responsibility for them.

Any people depicted in stock imagery provided by Thinkstock are
models, and such images are being used for illustrative purposes only.
Certain stock imagery © Thinkstock.

Lulu Publishing Services rev. date: 08/12/2016

BULLET NUMBER ONE,
ZERO SECONDS,
ZAPRUDER FRAME 155

The first projectile, which was initiated from the Dallas County Records Building, missed President John F. Kennedy and landed on the public lawn on the south side of Elm Street. Said trajectory was altered by a tree, whose branches and leaves were between the shooter and the intended target. Witnesses reported seeing Deputy Sheriff Buddy Walthers and members of the Dallas Police

Force combing the entire area to recover and classify the bullet as evidence.

Upon recovering the bullet, Deputy Sheriff Buddy Walthers allowed an unidentified man to pocket the bullet, which was never seen again and no explanation was given for the way the bullet was handled. There is a distinct possibility that the shell was manipulated to produce a bullet called a "sabot," which would allow the bullet to be deployed from a larger shell casing. This combination of a smaller bullet and a larger casing would allow the projectile to pack a larger, more powerful strike via its increased velocity. On the Dealey Plaza side of the rooftop of the Dallas County Records Building, a 30.06 shell casing was found in the 1970s, indicating the possible use of a sabot.

The ten-second kill zone began when the percussion of bullet number one blurred the Zapruder film at frame 155. The Zapruder film speed of 18.3 frames per second times ten seconds equals 183 frames. Frame 155 plus 183 frames equals 338 frames, which is when the last recorded bullet struck Governor John Connally.

BULLET NUMBER TWO,
ONE SECOND,
ZAPRUDER FRAME 173

Bullet number two grazed the tie J.F.K was wearing, producing a five millimeter in diameter horizontal tear from left to right.

BULLET NUMBER THREE, TWO SECONDS, ZAPRUDER FRAME 188

Bullet number three struck President Kennedy just below the Adam's apple and above the breastbone. The bullet had a similar horizontal path as that of bullet number two and came to rest on the right side of J.F.K's neck, between his earlobe and the top of his right shoulder. This brass bullet was longer than one inch in length and had a pointed tip, in contrast to Lee Harvey Oswald's, which had rounded tip.

Bullets number two and three were probably fired from the same .22 caliber fully automatic pistol equipped with a silencer, similar to the one carried by United States military operatives such as Francis Gary Powers.

In Zapruder frames 173–188, one to two seconds, it is noticed that William Greer, the 54-year-old limousine driver, is seen with his right arm extended to the right and rear, in the same motion exhibited in firing a pistol. Although the evidence could not be validated, there was a strong odor of gunpowder in the limousine; sleight of hand cannot be ruled out. This coincides with what was seen by several government agents as well as public citizens, which was that the driver shot JFK. He had his foot on the brake during the kill zone, keeping the limousine almost motionless, while the brake lights were on.

At this moment, the umbrella man pumped a black umbrella in the air and the dark complected man raised his right arm high in the air. The umbrella was open only during the time that the shots were fired.

In Zapruder frame 210, three seconds, the umbrella man is directly between JFK and the Stemmons Freeway sign.

When this alignment occurs, the umbrella man pumps the umbrella about two feet in the air and the dark complected man puts his fist in the air. In light of the fact that the shot was not only from a great height, but was complicated by the difficult angle, visual confirmation was an absolute necessity to insure that the target was indeed impacted.

After the assassination, the two men are seen seated together, while the dark complected man communicates on a walkie-talkie. The umbrella man, identified as Louis Witt, was interviewed and later released. The dark complected man was never located or identified.

After passing the triple underpass, the limo stopped for 30 seconds, and the running joke was "we do not want to drive too fast so as not to kill the President."

BULLET NUMBER FOUR, FOUR SECONDS,
ZAPRUDER FRAME 230

Bullet number four impacted J.F.K about six inches below the right shoulder and to the left of the spinal column. The autopsy report indicated the wound was 4 x 7 millimeters, with a downward angle of 21.3 degrees, which was larger than bullet number three with dimensions of 3 x 5 millimeters. The bullet was never found because the medical staff at Parkland Hospital probably unintentionally dislodged the bullet in the process of applying massage to the President's heart.

BULLET NUMBER FIVE,
4.5 SECONDS,
ZAPRUDER FRAME 237

Bullet number five entered Governor John Connally in the upper-right quadrant of his back, producing an entrance wound measuring 8 x 15 millimeters and a downward trajectory of 27 degrees. This entrance wound differed from both JFK's entrance wound, which was 4 x 7 millimeters and a downward trajectory angle of 21.3 degrees, and his throat wound of 4 x 6 millimeters. The Governor's exit wound was below his right nipple and measured five centimeters.

BULLET NUMBER SIX

Bullet number six struck the core molding of the limousine on the passenger side, where Agent Roy Kellerman was riding. During his testimony before the Warren Commission, Kellerman claimed that there were far more shots fired then the three shots alleged by the Warren Commission. The Commission did not follow up or report on this disclosure.

BULLET NUMBER SEVEN, NINE SECONDS, ZAPRUDER FRAME 313

Bullet number seven was fired by Jimmy "The Weasel" Fratianno, an excellent marksman, from the second story of the Dal-Tex building. This bullet hit JFK in the back of his head. Fratianno was part of a three-man team, which included a timer and a back-up man to dispose of any evidence.

Fratianno was arrested and whisked away in a police car, only to be released later without charge. Fratianno's pay was $109,000 in non-repayable loans.

BULLET NUMBER EIGHT, NINE SECONDS, ZAPRUDER FRAME 313

Bullet number eight was fired by Jack Lawrence, an expert marksman in the United States Air Force. Just one month before the assassination, using a bogus resume, he obtained a job as a car salesman at the Downtown Lincoln-Mercury Dealer, which was only two blocks from Dealey Plaza. On the day of the shooting, Lawrence failed to report to work .

Thirty minutes after the assassination, a disheveled Lawrence showed up at the dealership, visibly upset and agitated. He acted so suspiciously that the employees summoned the police, who picked him up and released him the same day. The Downtown Lincoln-Mercury car he was driving was later found at the grassy knoll, where he had abandoned it. Jack Lawrence was probably supplied with the same timer and back-up man as the other shooter behind the fence, John Roselli. This shot produced a wound above the President's left eye as described by Father Oscar Huber, Dr. Adolph Giesecke, Jr., and Dr. Marion Jenkins.

BULLET NUMBER NINE, NINE SECONDS, ZAPRUDER FRAME 313

Bullet number nine was fired by John Roselli, the second shooter behind the fence. It hit the right side of the President's head, throwing him to the left and into the back seat. It also blew out his brains, producing a large opening in the back of his head. The bullet used was probably a sabot. John Roselli and his timer escaped by utilizing a manhole behind the fence, while his back-up man disposed of the guns and shells.

John Roselli was involved in the distribution of liquor, and employed gang muscle to scam the motion picture industry by stock manipulation and extortion. In November 1963, it surfaced that he had worked with the CIA in the assassination plot against Cuba's Fidel Castro.

Only days before he was to testify about the Kennedy Assassination, his body was found in an oil drum off the coast of Florida in 1976. His compensation was $250,000 in 1966, but he did not collect the money.

BULLET NUMBER TEN, NINE SECONDS, ZAPRUDER FRAME 313

Using a pagoda as coverage, bullet number ten was fired by Eugene Brading from Kennedy's left side. He was part of the triangle of John Roselli and Jimmy "The Weasel" Fratianno who fired simultaneously, moving J.F.K's head and causing Eugene Brading to miss. Eugene Brading's shot hit the curb and its fragments hit James Tague.

Eugene Brading was one of the people wearing a hat marked with a huge X, who police had been directed to allow through the police lines. After the assassination, he was taken to the Dal-Tex Building where his driver's license was run and he was subsequently released.

BULLET NUMBER ELEVEN,
NINE SECONDS,
ZAPRUDER FRAME 313

Bullet number eleven was fired by an unidentified assailant from the south manhole in the triple overpass, impacting the sidewalk. This structure has since been paved over.

BULLET NUMBER TWELVE, TEN SECONDS, ZAPRUDER FRAME 338

Research indicates that bullet number twelve struck Governor Connally in the right wrist and continued into his thigh.

COMMUNICATION EXPERTS

The Adolphus Hotel, across from Jack Ruby's Carousel Club, housed the radio coordination center and headquarters for Major General Edward Lansdale. The CIA liaison for Secretary of Defense Robert S. McNamara, Major General Lansdale became the chief of operations of a project that escalated into a small war against Cuba. He was also chief of operations of a project that imprisoned farmers and farm workers in Vietnam. A disagreement concerning the Vietnam operation resulted in a fallout between JFK and Major General Edward Lansdale, which led to his discharge . The next sighting of Major General Edward was at Dealey Plaza, the day of the JFK assassination.

Jim Hicks, also housed at the Adolphus Hotel, was the radio coordinator at the time of the assassination. This was verified by court documents.

Before the assassination, there was a car cruising behind the fence with one man holding a walkie-talkie. The man who accompanied the umbrella man was seen holding a walkie-talkie, and talking into it immediately after the assassination.

PRE-ASSASSINATION ACTIVITY

Two hours before JFK was assassinated, a 23-year-old woman named Julia Mercer was driving west on Elm Street. She saw a young man remove a paper bag from a tool compartment and take the package to the grassy knoll. Julia Mercer pulled alongside the truck and locked eyes with the driver, who was of stocky build and had light brown hair. On her way to Fort Worth, Texas, she reported this encounter to a policeman. Early the next morning, the FBI came to her home and took her to the Dallas Sheriff's Department, where the FBI showed her various photos. She picked out pictures of two men, one of which had Jack Ruby's name written on the back. A few months before the JFK assassination, Carousel Club dancer, Shari Angel, was at the Adolphus Hotel in Dallas, where she saw Vice President Lyndon Baines Johnson and Jack Ruby together. Two months before the assassination, Madeline Brown, LBJ's long-time mistress, saw him alongside Jack Ruby at the Carousel Club.

POST-ASSASSINATION ACTIVITY

Immediately after the assassination, photographer Phil Willis saw Jack Ruby, with whom he was familiar, outside the Book Depository. He photographed him there, gave the photograph to government officials, but the photograph vanished into thin air.

It is not known if Jack Ruby planted the bullet at Parkland Hospital when the President died, but it was verified that he was there.

Jack Ruby integrated himself into the midnight Dallas press conference.

On the morning of November 23, 1963, Lee Harvey Oswald was scheduled to be transported to a maximum security cell at Dallas County Jail. The Dallas Police Department had helped Jack Ruby gain access to the basement of the Dallas Police Headquarters. It is from here that Jack Ruby lunged from behind the Dallas Police Officers to shoot and kill Lee Harvey Oswald.

LEE HARVEY OSWALD

Within minutes of the assassination, Deputy Sheriff Roger Craig arrived at the location where the bullet struck the curb of Elm Street. He heard a shrill whistle and then noticed a white male running from the Book Depository and jump into a light-colored Rambler station wagon. Later that day, Deputy Sheriff Craig heard that the city had the suspect in custody; he went to City Hall where the suspect was identified as Lee Harvey Oswald. Captain William

Fritz later took Deputy Sheriff Craig into his office where Lee Harvey Oswald was interrogated. Oswald stated the Rambler station wagon belonged to a friend, Ruth Paine, who was unconnected to the past proceedings according to Oswald. Deputy Sheriff Craig verified his presence in Captain Fritz's office by being photographed there with the caption, "The Homicide Bureau Office, under guard while Oswald was being interrogated." Lee Harvey Oswald stated that "his cover was blown."

Within approximately one minute of the assassination, motorcycle patrolmen Marion Baker, Depository Superintendent Roy Truly, and Mrs. Robert Reid, clerical supervisor at the depository, all verified Lee

Harvey Oswald was on the second floor at that time.

The powers that be, all the way down to LBJ, wanted the investigation of the assassination over instantly, no conspiracy theory. What went wrong? Lee Harvey Oswald was an intelligent man who suspected his role was just a patsy. He simply out-witted Jack Ruby, who was waiting for him outside the depository, and he escaped.

Lee Harvey Oswald scored 212 on his first Marine Corps test, rating him as a "fairly good shot." In 1959, he scored 191, rating him as a "rather poor shot." According to witnesses, he scored a lot of "Maggie's Drawers," which were complete misses. A Soviet intelligence officer, Yuri Nossenko, who defected in 1964, stated that Lee Harvey Oswald was an extremely poor shot.

Multiple facts clearly indicated Oswald's defection to the Soviet Union was staged. Either the CIA or the Office of Naval Intelligence arranged his travel going to and coming from the Soviet Union. A separate legal organization of the government, possibly functioning out of the White House without the President's knowledge or consent, formulated and executed a plan controlling him from the outset.

Lieutenant Colonel Allison G. Folsom indicated to the Warren Commission that Lee Harvey Oswald taught himself fluent Russian. However, Oswald's grade in the Armed Forces Practical Russian Text 21 confirms he was taught Russian by the U.S.

Government. When Oswald requested a passport to Russia in 1963, he was issued one within 24 hours. When he returned from Russia, Oswald was hired by Jagger, Stover, and Childs, a company involved in high security work, such as maps and photography. Oswald's assigned FBI number was S-179 and he was paid $200 per month. In 1977, Victor Marchetti, executive assistant to the CIA's Director, discovered a CIA "201," which revealed that Oswald was a CIA agent. The weapon owned by Lee Harvey Oswald was a Beretta.

LBJ

Secret Service Director John Rowley's relationship with LBJ went as far back as the 1940s, when the two friends served in the National Youth Administration under FDR. The planning of the JFK trip to Dallas resulted in lapses in the Secret Service's protocol. For example, agents who were close to the President were removed from their positions. In addition, the limousine speed of five miles per hour was well below the required speed of 40 miles per hour, especially at the 120 degree turn leading to Dealey Plaza.